JARREL JONES

IN CAMERA

The Ultimate Guide to Capturing the Perfect Shot, Learn Useful Tips and Tricks on How You Can Use Your Digital Camera to Take Perfect Photos

Descrierea CIP a Bibliotecii Naţionale a României
JARREL JONES
    IN CAMERA. The Ultimate Guide to Capturing the Perfect
Shot, Learn Useful Tips and Tricks on How You Can Use Your
Digital Camera to Take Perfect Photos / Jarrel Jones. – Bucharest:
Editura My Ebook, 2020
    ISBN

JARREL JONES

IN CAMERA

The Ultimate Guide to Capturing the Perfect Shot, Learn Useful Tips and Tricks on How You Can Use Your Digital Camera to Take Perfect Photos

My Ebook Publishing House
Bucharest, 2020

Contents

USING YOUR DIGITAL CAMERA PROPERLY

To improve the quality of every portrait that you take, you need to use your camera in the right way. Digital cameras are not like single use cameras. They are not always as complex as traditional, film cameras, either. They fit somewhere in between. Still, if you want to get a great picture, you do have to have the right tools to do the job. In fact, the biggest hold up most people have is not knowing the basics of how their camera works. This will slow you down considerably.

For those using an SLR camera, it will take some time to get used to the features. One of the features that you will benefit from right off the bad is the focus options. If you have an SLR camera, you should avoid using the auto focus setting. With a quality camera, you will have various focus options. Try them all. Learn how to choose the right one, based on your owner's manual in particular. This will improve the quality of your shot virtually every time.

You also should consider shooting in manual mode rather than automatic mode. Many people feel that the camera is smart enough to make the decisions for you and therefore use the automatic mode as often as they can. However, this can cause problems for you. Instead, invest some time in learning how to use the manual mode first. This will enhance your ability to be creative in your shots and more in control of the final photo.

White balance is another area that most people avoid. If you have an SLR camera, you have the ability to choose custom white balance (in most cases.) Try using various options here. You may want more color if you are in a location that is indoors. In the sun, you may want less. The key to remember here is that auto white balance really does not do anything. But, if you do take the time to adjust this and try out different methods, you could find yourself with a fantastic picture.

Invest some time in reading your owner's manual. Not only does it give you the step by step instructions for using your digital camera, but it will also give you tips on how to use your camera properly, to get the best finished photo. Experimentation is also one of the best ways to learn how to take the best shots every time.

PREPARING FOR GREAT LANDSCAPE SHOTS

One mistake people often make when taking photos of a landscape is rushing. There is no reason (yes no reason) to force this shot. You may be losing light or you may be missing your shot, but this comes from poor planning. Instead, invest the time in preparing for a great landscape shot. Many love landscapes. They are full of color, peace and often are very alluring. You may find them to be some of the most creative shots you ever take, if you learn to take them properly. You can do this!

Get Ready

First off, be ready for your trip. Here are some tips to prepare.

1. Be sure you have a quality tripod with you. Without a tripod, you will be unable to get a truly good quality shot off. Some of it will blur if you try to do it free hand. A quality tripod

should be easily mounted or freestanding and it should be sturdy!

2. Next, consider extra memory and batteries. The first shot is unlikely to be the best shot of the day. Sometimes, it takes a while to get your best shot.

3. Choose a good telephoto and wide-angle lens to use. You want to use the telephoto because it can give you great zoom on various images. You can get all of those interesting details that really make the landscape come to life. The wide angle lens will improve the scope of the photo, giving a panoramic feel to it.

Lighting

The next thing to think about is your lighting. Lighting is key to good photos. Most photographers prefer the light of the early morning hours or the sunset hours because it is farther away and therefore more diffused. The midday sun is simply too harsh and colors are lost because of it.

More Tips

Do not forget to find an interesting area to focus on and then to use that as the image's focal point. You do not want to let your viewer get lost in your shot. In addition, you do not want to center your photos. You want them to be off center, as this will create a more interesting scene for you.

Go ahead and practice because that, above all else, is going to give you the best landscape shots you can have. Most importantly, give yourself enough time to find the right shot by having plenty of time to change your mind.

TAKING GOOD STILL LIFE CAMERA SHOTS

For some of us, photography is more than just snapping some pictures once in a while. It is something that we enjoy doing and a way of expressing ourselves. Like with most types of art forms, the best way to improve is to learn and then practice, repeatedly. Though it is nice to have live subjects with which to practice our photography, working with still life can be a learning process all its own, and can be a great way to work with different effects. Also, with still life you have a variety of different subjects that you can work with; limited only by your imagination and what you have available.

Still life photography is a lot more difficult than many people realize. When you photograph people or animals it is much easier to capture a mood than when you are photographing inanimate objects. The challenge of creating a mood with still life photography is what can make it so exciting, though. By working with such things as light, shadow, focus and different backgrounds, you can take one still life subject and elicit completely different types of moods.

This is your objective; to use inanimate objects to inspire emotion in the viewer.

To practice your still life photography, you want to take a day when you can be undisturbed for a period of time. Find a spot that you can turn into a studio for a while, or if you really do have a studio, all the better. Think of various everyday objects that you can photograph, such as fruit, books, or small pieces of pottery. Start with one thing, because you're going to want to practice photographing it in different ways to try to create different moods. Then, start practicing. Choose a feeling that you want to create and start using lights and backgrounds to create that mood.

This is a wonderful way to exercise your creativity and imagination.

Think of your still life photography as telling a story. For instance, you can put some old books between two bookends and then place a brightly illustrated child's book open in front of them. By sharpening the focus on the old books and blurring it slightly on the child's book, you are portraying the importance of learning from past generations. By doing the opposite you are encouraging people to think of how life goes on, and how the old has to make way for the new. Open your mind to the ways that you can speak to others through your still life photography and you should be happy with the results.

TAKING THE BEST PICTURES FOR YOUR WEBSITE

When you have your own website, whether it is a business website or a personal website, you usually like to put some nice pictures on it. Having pictures on your website makes it more attractive to the people who are visiting it, and making your website attractive to visitors should be your goal. Especially if it is a business website where you are hoping that visitors will purchase your products or services, you want the pictures that you place on it to inspire the right feelings in your visitors. Even if the website does not revolve around a business, you still want the pictures to be pleasing to the eye.

When considering photos for your website, you want to think about how you want your website visitors to feel. Perhaps you have a business website and you are selling your own handmade hair clips. Of course, you want to display pictures of the various hair clips that you have to offer, but that is not enough to get people excited. You also want to show pictures of people wearing your hair clips. It is not enough to just do that, either. The girls or women wearing your hair clips should look like they are pleased to be wearing them. Perhaps you can get a shot of a woman wearing one of your hair clips and getting attention from a handsome man. You could also show a young girl wearing your hair clip and looking adorable in a party dress. Your goal is to create the right kind of emotions in your website visitors.

The great thing about putting pictures on your website is that it is very easy to put them on and take them off again. You often have to experiment with different types of pictures and get some feedback from other people before you decide what to keep on your website and what not to.

Most likely you'll be changing the pictures now and then as well. As you display different pictures and see the results that they bring you, you can adjust and modify continually.

Make sure that your pictures reflect the theme of your website. If you have created a website about responsible pet ownership, you might not want puppy and kitten pictures on there; it can conflict with the fact that you are trying to convince people to spay and neuter their pets. Make sure that your pictures flow well with the theme of your website and you will find that your visitors will stay longer and enjoy it more.

TAKING THE PERFECT EVENT PICTURES

When you are attending an event such as a New Year's Eve party, a wedding, or even just a child's birthday party, you often want to bring your camera to record the festivities. Taking pictures of an event, whether it is yours or someone else's, is a great way to remember it for posterity, and ideally you want to capture the mood of the event with your camera in the best way possible. When you put care and consideration into getting the best shots at an event you are doing yourself and everyone there are big favor. Some planning and attention to detail now can make for the most memorable shots.

Events are usually about milestones and celebrations, and each has a different and special mood. It is this mood that you want to capture when taking pictures. If you are at a wedding, you want to capture the love between the two people getting married, the pride and happiness that their parents feel, even the slight trepidation the best man feels as he observes the end of an era! This means that you want the majority of the pictures you take to be those in which the subjects don't know they're being photographed.

You want to capture the bride and groom exchanging a private look, the New Year's Eve party guest letting his hair down more than you've ever seen him do, the graduate clasping the hand and smiling at the person giving her the diploma. The rule when taking event pictures is to record the feeling, not the people. Though this may seem like you are not giving enough importance to the people who will be in the shots, the opposite is actually true. What better way to help people remember the emotions they felt during an event than to show them feeling the emotions rather than just smiling for the camera.

If you must take some shots that are posed, such as when a group wants their picture taken together, then try to get the people to be as animated as possible. Talk to them for a bit before taking the picture; get them to laugh and interact, and definitely get them to relax. Do what you can to distract them from the fact that they're getting their picture taken and you'll be able to get some group or individual shots that really stand out from the rest. When you put care and thoughtfulness into event pictures, you and your subjects are rewarded in some wonderful ways.

TAKING THE PERFECT PET SHOT

Most of us like to take and have pictures of our families, and this includes our four-footed family members as well. Often you can see people displaying pictures of their pets as proudly as they display pictures of their children. It can be difficult, however, to get pets to cooperate when we want to take their pictures, but there are some tricks that we can use to make the job a little easier. We can often get the best pictures of them by playing to their natures. Sometimes this means asking for a little help; one person taking the picture and one person working with the animal.

To get good shots of your dog, enlist the help of another person and have this person interact with the dog and try to elicit various reactions. Choose a setting that will show your dog off in the best light, and use your zoom often to capture your dog's mood. Use a camera with a shutter speed that will allow you to get clear action shots. Have your helper try to inspire the best facial expressions and body language shots. This can include encouraging the dog to tilt his head when curious, lift his head high with ears up in an alert pose, or stand with chest down on the ground and hindquarters up in the air in a playful posture.

Cats are, of course, a different story. To get the best pictures of your cat you should also enlist someone's help. Since cats never concern themselves with pleasing their owners, you have to watch your cat's moods and take advantage of the times when he is feeling playful or particularly amiable. When the time is right, have someone help you get good shots by bringing out your cat's favorite toys and enticing the cat to play. If you want more of a portrait shot, try to get your cat comfortable in the setting that you want to shoot him in, and then wait for the right shot. Understand that you'll be working on his timetable, not yours.

Pets could care less about having their pictures taken, so it's up to you to set up an environment for them that will help you get the best shots. Pester them too much with a camera and they'll start to see it as something to avoid, so keep the camera out of their sight as much as possible. If you can't avoid having them see the camera, try to associate it with something good such as their favorite treats or toys. Cater to what your pets like and you'll be rewarded with memorable pictures.

TAKING VACATION CAMERA SHOTS

When we take a vacation, we like to record it with a camera so we can look at pictures and relive the moments again and again. Often we don't give much thought to how we take those pictures, though. We see something that interests us and take a quick picture of it, or we get our friends or family together, tell them to say cheese, and snap a quick shot. If you stop and think about it, though, your vacation memories are priceless, and you should take the time and effort to make the pictures of it priceless as well. Fortunately, it isn't that difficult.

The first thing that you want to make sure of is that you bring a good camera along on your vacation. Digital cameras work well because you can see right away whether the shot you've taken is what you want. Try to bring a camera that has a decent zoom feature so that you aren't limited in the types of pictures that you can take on your vacation. Depending on where you are vacationing, you often want to get in some good panoramic shots of the scenery, not just close up shots of people.

The one thing to keep in mind when taking vacation pictures is that you want to capture the mood and excitement of the trip. If you are taking your children to a major amusement park, for example, most of your pictures will probably be of them. Instead of having them stand and pose for you, though, you want to get pictures that capture their awe when they look at the things around them or their glee when on a ride. Go beyond this even, and catch your child's face at the end of the day, tired and maybe even a little cranky, but full of happy memories. Don't be afraid to catch more than just people smiling; catch all of the moods during your trip. It makes for more vivid memories.

When you take the time to really put some thought into your vacation pictures, you are doing yourself and the people you vacation with a great service. It will invoke a lot more emotion and vivid memories to look at a photograph of your spouse gazing at the vastness of the ocean from the rail of a cruise ship than if he is just standing there smiling for you. Taking the extra time to make your vacation pictures memorable will help you hold on to the wonderful feelings for years to come.

TAKING YOUR OWN PORTRAIT CAMERA SHOTS

Most people believe that to get a sitting portrait of their family, their children, or whatever else they want a portrait of, they need to seek the services of a professional. Though professional portrait takers usually do have quality equipment and studios, the fact is that it is possible for you to take your own portrait shots, and you can do it well. All it takes is a little understanding of the look you are trying to achieve and how best to achieve it. When you're using a digital camera, you have the luxury of being able to practice over and over again, or for as long as your subjects will agree to sit for you.

Look at a professional portrait picture. Make note of where the light and shadows are, what is in the background and how the subjects are centered. Pay attention to as many details as possible and try to emulate them to a degree while still using your own props. You will need some type of backdrop for your portrait. One of the most important aspects of a portrait shot is that the focus is completely on the subject. Even though some professional portrait shots show a photo background such as a beach or meadow, you can see that great care is taken to draw the eye to the subject at all times.

To begin with, you should probably use a solid background. You can use a solid wall, as long as it does not have anything on it like pictures or clocks. You can even use a projection screen as a background if you have one. Once you have found your background, your next step is to figure out where your subject will be sitting or standing. Once again, look at how professional photographers sit their subjects, but try to use your own creativity.

The more you practice taking portrait camera shots, the more you'll learn about what looks good and what doesn't. You will start getting your own unique ideas about how to portray your subjects, and you will be able to get their input in addition, about what they want. When you are taking your own portrait pictures you are not restricted to what a professional has to offer, and that gives you some artistic freedom. If you start slowly, practicing with one adult subject, you'll build the confidence to try other things like group portraits or baby portraits. You'll realize that there will always be room for more creativity, which will always make it an interesting hobby.

TIPS FOR CAPTURING A GREAT LANDSCAPE

You would like to take a few landscape shots and perhaps sell them or use them in some way. You have a great camera, but what about the landscape. You can find landscapes everywhere, even in a rural city or the most urban of cities. The key is capturing them in the right way. There are many things to consider, including the lighting, the type of film or camera you will use and even the focus you use. However, what about the landscape itself, it too should be carefully considered to pull off this shot.

There are several ways you can improve the quality of these shots. It all comes down to choosing the right landscape and then being read for it. If you planned to rush in this area, you are likely to ruin your shot. Instead, consider these quick tips.

1. Do invest in planning ahead of time. What will the weather be like? Is it going to give you the best shot? You can

shoot on cloudy days or those days that have amazing clouds. Even storms can be shot. But, you need to prepare with the right type of camera and focus. Look for a party cloudy sky if you want a great, full of color sunset!

2. Why not go for something unique, like taking a landscape picture that is lit by the moonlight? You can do this and it will give you a dramatic picture. To pull it off, you will need to get your exposure down right. You will want to have a longer exposure since the moonlight will nearly require it.

3. When capturing a sunrise or a sunset, keep in mind that you may get a dusty, or dirty, look. This is because of the farther distance that the sun's light has to travel to get that coloring. Still, for the most dramatic of shots you do have to go for sunrise or sunset. The colors are truly amazing especially at different times of the year.

Do invest in time. You will need time to get the right shot. Do not arrive last minute and hope the first shot you take is going to pull it off. Rather, step back and give yourself more time. It will pay off with a better, more planned shot. The colors, composition and lighting will be just right.

Landscape pictures are slow, carefully planned shots.

TIPS FOR DIM LIGHTING SHOOTING

Sometimes, poor lighting or dim lighting can be one of the best ways to color your photo. If you use it properly, you could have an amazing looking photo by the time you have your photo complete. Low light is a unique scenario, but it does give you the ability to be more creative in each of the shots you take. Keep in mind, it can take some practice to get these shots right.

The first thing to focus on is focus itself. You need quality focus. If you shoot your photos in the largest aperture (shooting wide open as it is called), you will have a depth of field that is rather shallow. Focus is critical in this scenario. When you are in this type of situation, pick a point of focus. The object of your focus needs to be carefully maintained. For example, in dim light, if you are shooting people, you want their eyes to be the point of sharp focus. Focus the eyes for the best final picture.

Next, consider movement. You are often told that movement in photos is a bad thing. However, you can make it work for you. In a situation in which there is movement, but you still want to get the best you can out of the photo, it is best to use movement to your advantage. The first thing to do is to capture using the best stability you can. For example, holding your camera as still as possible. One way to do this is to hold the camera as high as you can over your head, for example, if you are taking photos of a moving vehicle. You have stability. Then, take several shots at one time. Keep going until you get a good number of shots. You may be able to get them to six shots in just a few seconds. That will give you a great quality of shot even with movement.

Dim lighting situations can be bad, if you do not have the right type of gear to work with them. For example, if you have just the on board flash, you may need to minimize this better by using a diffuser of some sort for your flash. Even with a mediocre camera, you can get great shots even when your lighting is not perfect. Use this dim light to your advantage. You may even want to practice in it to learn how to use it.

TIPS FOR USING A SELF TIMER
FOR BETTER PICTURES

To get great looking pictures, it is often important to have a steady hand. What if you are struggling with this area though, it happens all too often. In fact, many people will have trouble getting that perfectly still shot. One way to get around this is to use a self timer or a remote to control when the picture is taken. If you can keep your hands off the camera, you likely can have better looking pictures.

What Is A Self Timer?

Many cameras, especially digital cameras, are now designed to incorporate a self timer. Just like any other timer, when activated, the timer begins to tick down. When it gets to 0, it will trigger the shutter to go off, taking your picture for you. In cameras, this can be very important to have because it gives you the ability to take pictures with yourself in them or to take pictures that are steady, even shots.

Here's how to use a self timer well.

1. Read the manual from your camera to learn the particular way of activating the self timer on your camera. Some are a bit different from others in how they work, too.

2. Set up your shot. Even if you just are getting a group together, do invest the time in doing this. Align everyone properly. Place the camera on a flat, steady surface other than in your hands.

3. Press down on the keys to activate the timer. You may need to hit the shutter button after this to tell the camera what to do.

4. The timer will begin to count down. It usually only gives you about ten to fifteen seconds and then will take the picture.

5. Leave the camera alone for about five to ten seconds after the picture has been shot. Check it out, if digital to make sure you got the shot.

Another similar option is the remote control. If you have upgraded your camera to include one, they work in a similar way. What is nice about these is that you can easily use them for any of the pictures you wish to take by setting the camera up and snapping the shot from any distance you are in.

Using these features on a digital camera is the best way to get the best shot. When quality matters and you do not want the blur of movement, do invest in these methods.

TIPS FOR SUCCESSFUL DIGITAL CAMERA SHOTS

Prior to the ease of use of digital cameras, photographers (no matter what experience level they were) had to spend a great deal of time taking photos. They had to take several different pictures of the same pose, with the hopes of getting the right shot. Today, with the use of digital cameras, it has gotten easier because you get an instant view of the shot you just took. Still, that does not means that every shot you take will be a good one.

There are differences when using SLR and DSLR cameras that you need to get used to. What happens when you get a poor picture is happening within the makeup of the camera. These cameras have a separate lens for different resolutions. This helps to give the camera the ability to work well at diversified depths. To do this, these cameras use light sensor chips and digital memory.

To get better at taking great shots with this type of camera, you have to do the good old thing and practice at it. You will need to keep trying various methods until you get a feel for the way the camera works. Sometimes there is a delay, which will slow you down. Other times, you may get a blurred look just from the slightly movement of your hand.

Some tricks that can help you include these:

• Take a closer up photo. This will help you to get a clearer picture and it helps to keep the pictures from looking small. Because the camera has the ability to take a longer-range shot, does not mean you should always use this.

• Invest in a quality camera and do read through the owner's manual. There are going to be various settings to learn, including various focuses. The better you know these, the better the final look will be.

• Watch the white balance on the camera. If you are taking shots outside, for example, you need to set the white balance on the camera to cloudy instead of keeping it on auto.

Digital camera shots can be hard to get if you have never used these cameras in the past. Once you learn how to use them, though, you will likely not want to go back to using traditional cameras. The ease of use and the ability to know that you have the best picture makes all of the difference with these cameras.

USING LIGHT AND SHADOW TO ENHANCE PHOTOS

Almost everyone likes to take pictures now and then, but for some of us it becomes a hobby and often a passion. Taking photographs can be a way of recording events in our lives, but it can also be an art. One of the ways that you can enhance the pictures you take is by manipulating light and shadows in order to get different effects. Though we always have to take light conditions into consideration when we are taking pictures, we don't often think about making them work for us instead of trying to work with them. When you start using light and shadow to enhance and manipulate your photos, you often seem some surprising and delightful results.

Using light and shadow to get the effect that you want often involves using artificial light. You see examples of this all the time when you watch a photographer at work in a studio. The photographer will use lights that are large, small, bright, or dim to change how you see the subject. Some of the lights will be completely uncovered and some will have backs that can be moved around to change the direction of shadows. Often when we look at professional model or still-life photos we aren't even aware of how much light and shadow manipulation has gone into them.

When you are taking pictures outside you don't have as much control over the light and shadows as you would in a studio, but this doesn't mean that you can't work with them for photo enhancement. When you know how certain places look at certain times of the day, you can schedule pictures for when the light and shadows will work best for you. You can wait until sunset to get a silhouette of your subject against a softly glowing ocean, or shoot a picture at noon so that you have the sun directly above your subject for maximum light.

If you are just learning how to manipulate light and shadow to get different photographic effects, it can help to construct some type of makeshift studio where you can practice. Rather than annoy live subjects as you practice, start with inanimate objects. Purchase or construct your own photography lights using different shades and wattage, and start experimenting by using different light angles on one subject. You'll be surprised at how easily you change the look of something, and you are likely to become hooked on light and shadow enhancement photography.

A FEW THINGS THAT ARE MUSTS
FOR THE PHOTOGRAPHER

No one wants to take a lot of equipment with them when they leave the house, but there are some items you may want to keep at your disposal if you are planning to take great photos while you are out and about. Perhaps you are heading to the beach with the family. You may be going to the park to capture some great photos for your collection. Whatever you do, you need to invest in having the right equipment to ensure every shot counts.

The Things You Need

So, what should you have ready to go? Here are a few things everyone should have if they are out shooting.

1. Multimedia Photo Viewers: It happens to everyone: the filled up memory without warning. If you are out shooting, these

photo viewers are a great investment because they allow you to transfers your photos from your camera. There are several different configurations and they will cost you a few hundred dollars, but for a photographer that wants to have maximum options, these photo viewers are the way to go.

2. Look for a flexible tripod. A good example of this is a Gorilla pod. What is nice about them is they are highly sturdy and very easy to use. You can place them on just about anything. Mount them to your bike or even to something you come across on your shoot for some interesting shots. They are not too expensive, usually under $100 and are very easy to transport from place to place. Get the right size for your camera, though.

3. The Diffuser. A diffuser can help you to improve the coloring and reduce the intensity of your flash. Depending on if you have invested in a high expensive and hard to use external flash, you may want to choose another option. For example, you can use a white card placed at an angle at the flash to allow the diffuser against something else, such as the wall. Or, you can use a piece of scotch tape over the flash. You will need to work with it to get the best results.

When it comes to shoots like this, you should be ready for anything. These tips will help you ensure you are ready for all those shots that are important to you. Even for a planned event, having these pieces with you can save the day or at least save the shot.

BETTER PICTURES BY FOCUSING ON COMPOSITION

For those who are hoping to improve the quality of their shots, there are many ways to make this happen, including paying a bit of closer attention to the composition of the shot. The composition is comprised of everything that is in the photo. This includes your subject, which is the person or thing that is your main goal in the picture. In addition to this, all of the background the foreground and anything to the side of the subject is part of the composition. Getting the composition right is an important part of succeeding in improving your photos.

The Common Mistake

One of the biggest mistakes made with composition is not paying attention to what else is in the photo when you are taking it. For example, many people often look only at the subject of their photo, not paying attention to whom else or what else is in the picture. An example of this is taking a quick shot of your family at an amusement park. You pull out the camera and want to get the shot fast to capture their happiness. So, you look for them in the lens, hope they are smiling and take the photo. The result is either a blurred shot from rushing or it has some stranger in the background, who you did not want to be there.

Rather than doing this, stop and invest just a few extra seconds in the shot. Here is a rundown to look for.

1. Is the subject centered and as close as possible? Fill them up with the shot to get the best result.

2. Look at the background. Who is there? Is there are a trash can right next to them or anything else that is less than appealing? If so, move the shot so that you avoid these items.

3. Is the zoom right? If there is something in the photo that you do not want to be there, it is best to zoom in and avoid that. You may be able to crop this out later, but if it is an important element in the photo, you may need to change the scenery of the entire shot.

Paying a bit more attention to the composition of the photos you take only takes an investment of a few extra seconds. When you do so, you will capture amazing, high quality photos that are not lacking in substance.

CAPTURING NATURE WITH YOUR CAMERA

Taking pictures of nature can be very rewarding, and is a great way to share with others how you felt being out in it. When you are taking pictures out in nature, however, you want to follow certain guidelines so that you can capture the feel in the best way possible. This means working with nature instead of trying to control it, and doing your best to portray its various moods. The best nature pictures are those that you take when you have immersed yourself in the beauty and wonder around you.

When capturing nature on camera, you often want to get some far away or panoramic shots, such as of snow-capped mountains or a lake and meadow. This means that you will want to have a good quality zoom feature on your camera. When taking these types of panoramic shots, try to get enough in to capture the beauty and splendor of what you see. A shot that has almost all lake in it with just a little bit of grass doesn't do the whole scene justice. You want to get a nice part of the lake with enough meadow to show how they interact together, and perhaps a mountain or some trees in the background.

Taking pictures of nature means trying to get others to see what you are seeing. This is why you want to get the lake, the meadow, and at least part of a mountain in the shot. It also means being patient with wild animals that you want to photograph. If you know that a certain meadow is visited often by deer for grazing, make yourself comfortable near the meadow and wait.

Construct a blind if you have the resources so that you can be sure none of the animals will be able to see you. Be patient, make sure your camera and the zoom feature is ready, and you could end up with some wild animal pictures worthy of framing.

Though a lot of the time you don't really want people in your nature shots, there are times when it can actually enhance the picture. If you are on a hike with a friend, try to get some candid shots of her inspecting a certain plant or gazing out at a particularly beautiful natural scene.

Make the focus of your picture how your friend is reacting to the nature around her, not just a picture of your friend. Remember that when you let nature set the tone, which is when you get your best shots.

DOES DEPTH OF FIELD MATTER TO PICTURE QUALITY?

As you enhance your skills as a photographer, you will want to choose various ways to improve the quality of each photo you take. One area where you may be able to enhance the quality is in the depth of field. This term stands for the area that is in the photo in sharp focus. If you look at any picture and imagine it on different planes, you will notice that only one pane of the photo is actually in real, true focus. The rest cannot be. This is commonly assumed in photos. But, you can alter this depth of field to get a different perception and often create a very unique photograph.

To change the depth of focus, you will need to learn a few things about your lens. In particular, you will need to change the aperture of the lens. This term means the focal length of your lens or the distance from the lens to the subject. If you would like to get very advanced in these changes, learn more about the circle of confusion in photography and the hyper-focal distance. Still, without going into those details, consider these pointers.

First, there is not one way that is right 100 percent of the time in terms of depth of focus. Rather, you can choose what you wish to focus on. You can be more artistic or more traditional in this application. It is up to you. One creative choice is to choose some images to have a very narrow depth of focus while others have a very wide depth of focus. Let's say you are taking a photo of a car. You will want a wider depth of focus so that from the front to the rear, the car is in full view. On the other hand, perhaps you are taking a photo of a person eating an ice cream cone. You probably want a more shallow depth of focus so that the person's face is nice and sharp.

To make these chances, you have several options. You can switch out your lens focal length. Or, you can simply move your stance farther away or closer. You can also change the aperture of the lens. The key is to be creative. Try out different depth of field options until you actually get used to the different options you have. The key is to learn how to change the depth of field to match your composition.

DOES THE CAMERA MATTER?

Everyone wants to have a better-looking shot when it comes to his or her photographs. Your goal is to get the best shot you can get, but doing so is at the mercy of the camera, right? If you are a beginner you do not have to go out and purchase an expensive camera and assume that, it is going to give you all that you need. On the other hand, do not assume that the simple point and shoot camera is going to give you perfectly clear photos every time. Instead, you need to find a middle ground.

The Camera Is Part Of It

The camera you use is part of it. When you first start out, take some time to choose the right camera. Choose based on how you will use it. Will you be taking photos that you plan to sell? If so, you will need a very high quality, multi faceted camera. On the other hand, if your goal is simply to take family photos (which really are just as important) you may want to choose a friendlier version. The complexity of the camera is only as good as the user.

Use reviews to help you to select the right camera. It is often best to try an SLR digital camera, which allows you to do more of the controlling of the picture. A point and shoot camera will not give you as many options, including options such as flash control and auto focus. You will want these if at all possible.

You Matter Too

To get the perfect shot, you cannot make the mistake of believing that the camera is all to blame. You also need to take into consideration your abilities. If you have not taken the time to learn how to take great shots, chances are good you will be unable to do so. Take the time to read the owner's manual. This will give you all the details you need including how to use each of the features the camera offers and when to use them. Most cameras come with much more than just a how to manual. They give you details.

The right camera is an important part of taking great pictures. Still, you are an integral part of the process too. Keep in mind the importance of quality skills. Learn how to use your camera and most importantly, make the right investments in your time (you do need to learn how to be creative with your shots!)

FLASH BLOW OUT: AVOIDING IT

Flash blow out is actually common. It is a problem that many individuals have who are unfamiliar with using their camera or have little experience taking great quality photos. You can improve this though. Flash blow out happens when a room is darker or otherwise poorly lit and the picture that results is virtually impossible to see. In other words, the flash on your camera completely ruined the subject of the shot. The subject of the shoot is usually surrounded by bright light. You can avoid this though.

One of the first steps in improving flash blow out so you can avoid the problem is by stepping back. You may have been taught that you should be as close to your subject as possible, so that you fill up the entire space with your subject. This is good advice, but not in a poorly lit room. The closer you stand to the subject, the more blurry and bright they will be. Rather, step back and instead zoom in on the subject. This will disburse some of the light throughout the room (from the flash) keeping the subject properly lit.

Another way to avoid that flash burnt out look is to bounce the flash. This process involves causing the light from the flash to bounce off another surface before it hits your subject. The problem with this is that most point and shoot cameras do not give you the ability to do this. So, you have to be a bit more creative to make it happen. Use a white, small card in front of the flash. Angle it up or towards a wall so that the light has to bounce off that surface before it hits your subject. Always ensure you use a white card, otherwise, any color on the card will end up showing up in the picture as it will change the color of the light you use.

Flash burn out is a problem for most digital camera users in this poorly lit situation. Take the time to light the room properly, if it is possible to do so, so that you can avoid the need for using these tips. If you can't do that, invest a bit more time in taking the shots. That way, you have the ability to get a fantastic shot, even when the situation is not perfect. Most cases will result in no bright lights surrounding your subject, then.

GETTING THE BEST CAMERA SHOTS AT NIGHT

For many people, taking pictures at night simply means using a flash. They don't give it much more thought than that. If you are a photography buff, though, you might think differently about nighttime photography. To you they can be a way to show your passion for photography; a unique and beautiful form of expression. There are tricks to taking good night pictures; tricks that involve more than just using a decent flash to light up your subjects. Depending on the mood that you are trying to evoke, your night pictures can be exciting, calming, sexy, or inspiring.

Night pictures need a certain amount of light, of course. What is special about them, though, is that the light can be an integral part of the mood you want to create with your photo. If you are at an outdoor summer pool party, for example, you can get some wonderful pictures of people by the pool. When you find just the right angle you can use the light at the bottom of the pool to illuminate only one part of a person's face, giving an ethereal look to the shot. The reflection of the moon on a lake or the ocean can make the simplest photo suitable for framing.

Night photographs can be tricky. It often takes a lot of practice to learn the subtleties of light and shadow at night, and at first you'll find yourself discarding more photos than you keep. When photographing people's faces, red-eye is often a problem, but this problem can often be dealt with by manipulating the light sources so that they don't "attack" your subject too harshly. One way to do this is to not use your camera's flash, but to use a bright enough light source that is farther away from your camera. This is also a great way to get different effects.

Whether you are taking pictures of people or things, you want to capture the special feel that nightfall adds to the atmosphere. When taking a picture of a lake in the moonlight you want people to think that they can almost hear the crickets chirping. When taking a picture of a city at night you want to capture the excitement and anticipation. Play with the lights at night; don't be afraid to let them streak a bit for effect, or get an angle so that one thing is illuminated more than others. You'll find that night photography gives you ample opportunity to use your imagination and creativity in wonderful ways.

GETTING THE RIGHT SHOT FOR MONEY

There has always been a photographer out to make money off the shots he or she takes. As an artist, you want people to enjoy what you are shooting and there is no reason why you can't earn some money at it in the process. The key here is to create photos that people want to buy. You can do this rather easily by simply investing in the right shots. What does it take to create a great shot for the money?

Tips To Help You

Several things will help you to get more for your photos. It starts with knowing how to shoot. The most important thing you can do is to learn about your camera's abilities. Invest time in reading the owner's manual and testing out photos. People expect interesting and unique photos and they want quality. Therefore, to get this, you need to know how to use the features on your camera that can create it. It is not always easy to do, but it will be fun to learn!

Next, learn something about photos. You should understand when to use light and how to use light. You should learn how to use focus and how to use your modes. Automatic really should not be used in this type of quality shot. You need to be more creative and definitely have the ability to properly focus your shots. If lighting is not right, the entire impact of the photo will be lost.

What else can you do to get the most money from your perfect shots? Be creative. Learn to play with depth of field. Find out how to focus your pieces so that they are different from others. Of course, anyone purchasing photos will expect them to be very sharp in focus. This will determine if they can use them. Having a good quality camera capable of producing this type of quality is also important.

If you will be taking portraits, have a camera that is able to offer you the right lens. You may also want to consider having a larger, wide lens if you will target landscapes. Learn how to use your tripod. Get creative as to where you mount the tripod to get interesting shots. Most importantly, be sure that your subject comes through loud and clear. If you want someone to buy from you, be sure that the subject of your photos is as easy to depict as possible.

GETTING THE PERFECT SHOT
WITHOUT A TRIPOD

A tripod is an excellent tool to have if you will be taking photos in one location. They are far from practical, though, for most other instances. Yet, the problem that many people have with using cameras is the "camera shake" that often occurs when they take photos without this tool.

Camera shake often results in blurry pictures, sometimes not noticeable until your pictures are printed.

One of the best ways to avoid the camera shake is to adjust the camera shutter speed. Since this needs to react fast enough to overcome any movement, it can be very valuable to choose a shutter speed that is better. Let us explain through an example. If you are taking hand held shots with your camera, you may want to change the shutter speed to make it the equivalent to the focal length of the lens. An example of this is this: if you are using a

50 mm lens, you do not want your shutter speed to be anything less than 1/50th of a second, with faster being a better option.

There are a few other tips that can help you. For example, if you are taking a camera shot with your hands, use both hands instead of one. This gives the camera more stability. You are less likely to move it. The added stabilization of the camera will help you to improve the shot tremendously. Try to keep your elbows on either side of your body. This too will improve the stabilization.

Place the camera in your hands. Position your elbows properly. Then, prior to taking the shot, steady your hands. Keep your eyes on your subject. Loosen your grip so you are less likely to be moving the camera when it shoots. When you do hit the shutter, do your best not to move the camera for about five seconds after it flashes. Often it is necessary to do this to keep the shot from blurring. A good way to keep the picture looking great is to get positioned, then take a deep breath. Then, press the shutter. After you press the shutter, exhale.

Of course, it does take time to perfect such a shot. It is never easy to get the right shot all the time, either. It can take some time to get just what you are looking for. Having a quality camera also makes a big difference in the quality of the shot.

HOW TO BE AN EXPERT BEHIND THE CAMERA

There are countless times when people will say, "wow, look at the detail and color in that photograph." They do not often ask who the photographer is, though. The picture is the expert here, it is what defines an expert from an amateur. You do not need to have extensive training to pull off a great picture, though. The best thing you can do is to know enough about cameras and the usage of them to create a stellar photo. Here are some tips to help you to always create the very best shot you can in any circumstance.

1. Choose the composition properly. Look at everything that is involved in your photo. You do not want something negative at the side or behind your subject to ruin the otherwise perfect picture.

2. Focus in on one thing. If you are taking a landscape shot or even a portrait, you need to choose just one thing to

focus on. In a landscape of a mountain, it may be a small peak that you focus on. In a portrait, be sure that the eyes are focused.

3. Learn how to use your flash! This is a big deal in today's photography world because so many people flip their camera to auto focus and believe that the camera will do all the work for them. This is a mistake. Instead, learn how to use the various flash options you have and adjust them as you need to.

4. Do not allow your lens to auto focus, either. Just like your flash, you want to learn how to use various lens and various focus types. This can help you to enhance your photos and be more creative.

5. Learn to use light. Of all of these things listed here, light can ruin them all if it is not perfectly selected. When choosing the right amount of light, keep in mind you can control it. For example, place a white card in front of the flash angled to the ceiling to diffuse the flash and give your subject a bit less of the harsh flash light.

Learn how to use your camera. To be the expert is to create the perfect pictures. You can only accomplish this if you invest in some training. You can train yourself, but to do so, you do need to invest in time practicing. Practice is often what makes the perfect shots happen.

IMPROVING PORTRAIT PICTURES

If you wish to improve your ability to take portrait shots, one of the first things you need to do is to ensure you are concentrating on the person, rather than on the picture itself. A portrait should capture a person in a still position, but it should capture more than just what they look like. It should be a representation of who they are. This is not always easy to do, especially when your subjects are not as willing as they should be. Still, your goal is to capture the look, traits, and even the frame of mind of the subject in these shots.

How can you improve the quality of your portrait shots so that every picture you take really hits the target goal? It will take time, but these tips should help you to improve your portrait pictures.

1. Learn about lighting. Lighting is an important part of any portrait. Imagine a small child, with a heavenly glow, for example. It plays an important part in pulling off the quality of

this shot. You should learn about the chief glow, which is the light that is usually located about 45 degrees to the left or to the right of the subject.

2. Know your subject. Ask questions and get to know your subject. It is often best if the subject answers the questions himself or herself. The reason for this is quite simple. When you get them talking about something they are passionate about, their expression will match their thoughts. Capturing this frame of mind is important to getting a great finished photo.

3. Invest the time in the right shot. While most photographers are busy, it goes without saying that if you invest quality time in making the shot happen, it will more than likely happen successfully. It can take some time to develop the skills to take quality portraits, but working the picture with various lighting and focus options will improve the result.

It is easy to over think the portrait process. You do not want a strained picture as this lacks the character and emotion that should be present in these shots. From well back into the middle of the 19th century, people have wanted a portrait of themselves that captures who they truly are. The mark of a successful photographer is being able to pull this off successful. Improving portrait pictures you take will take time but it does pay off.

PERFECT CAMERA SHOTS – GETTING CHILDREN AT THEIR BEST

We love to take pictures and have pictures taken of our children. When they are young we take them to portrait studios or wait excitedly for their class pictures each year, and we keep cameras handy to snap photos of them at every opportunity. Sometimes the pictures look wonderful and sometimes they leave something to be desired. There is a way, however, to take your own high quality, memorable pictures of the children in your family, or any children you wish to photograph; pictures that will be even more precious than any professional portrait.

You need to use a good quality camera, and it must have a good zoom feature. Most people prefer digital cameras these days, and there are advantages to using them. When you take pictures with digital cameras you can see them right away, which lets you know if you are getting what you want or if you need to change any details. You will need the zoom because you will be taking pictures of the children as they are going about their days, preferably unaware that they are being photographed. You want to schedule a day for taking these photos. Dress the children in nice but appropriate outfits for where they will be photographed.

Wait for the right day and take your children somewhere where they are most likely to be happy and animated, such as a park. Since one person will be manning the camera and will want to be a good distance away from the child or children, another person will have to be there to watch the children closely for safety reasons. Ideally, you don't want to tell the children that any photography will be going on, in order to ensure that they will be acting completely natural. Let them loose to do what they do best, and start snapping away, using the zoom lens on a regular basis to get facial expressions and close interactions.

When you photograph children this way you are recording them being themselves; not acting out because they think someone is taking their picture. You'll be delighted at some of the shots you can get; completely natural facial expressions and body language. There will be a noticeable difference in these photographs. You don't have to worry about getting it right the first time, either. There are always things that can go wrong, but there will also be plenty of chances to improve.

Printed by Libri Plureos GmbH in Hamburg,
Germany